Poetry

A Fuzzy-Fast Blur

Poems about Pets

by Laura Purdie Salas

Capstone press

Mankato, Minnesota

2

Slobbery

Some think I wear a constant frown

It's just my tongue that weighs me down!

I love to loll and pant and drool

And form a swishy, foamy pool

Of spit that I can not keep in!

It makes me smile a happy grin.

I have a lot of tongue, it's true. . .

Shall I share a lick with you?

3

CAT-ching Up on Our Rest

It's been a long and busy day
It's passed by in a blur
It started when you scratched our necks
and stroked our silky fur
You could tell we liked that by
our deep and rumbly purr

You told us we're your favorite pets
(Of course, we knew we were)
It's two sweet cats or slobbering dogs
Who else could you prefer?
But now we're tired of being loved
We're much too sleepy to stir

Perched on Me

You stare in the mirror

And eat wicker baskets

And mimic me blowing my nose!

You're noisy and messy

But, still, you're my favorite. . .

As long as you don't bite my toes!

Softness

faithful furry friend:
you cuddle my happiness,
cushion my sadness

Come in,
Come in!

I'll make it easy
I'll open wide
I'll hope that you
will slide inside

Snakes eat mice
Some find that sad
But here's the truth:
They don't taste bad!

11

Friendship Skills:
Lesson 1

A guinea pig nibbled her carrot.

Another said, "Stop! I can't bear it!

I hate to be rude,

But my belly needs food!"

So the first pig agreed she would share it.

Glowing
Orange
Lacy
Delicate
Fanning
Iridescent
Shimmering
Hoverer

13

A Closer LOOk

bundle of energy
slick streak of fur
I race and I climb
a fuzzy-fast blur

14

I burrow, I chew things
I crawl and I leap
exhaustion takes over

I'm

    ready

        to

          . . .

Flat-Out Ferret

Very Scary Hairy Pet

It's true my tarantula's terribly hairy
She's grey like a shadow; she's Halloween-scary

I like that my spider looks gruesome and tough
'Cause now both my parents stay out of my stuff!

Reach

turtles
stretching, craving
shining sunlamp's glow
dry wrinkled skin soaking up warmth
basking

18

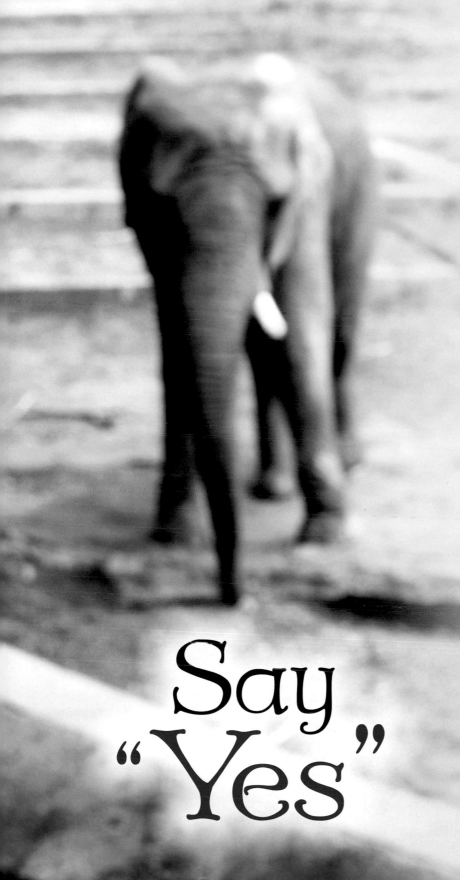

You said no to the orca
    Our bathtub's too small
And no to the stallion
    He needs his own stall

You said no to the spider
    Those long hairy legs!
And no to the tortoise
    She digs to lay eggs

You said no to the tiger
    He eats bloody meat
And no to the skunk
    She smells like old feet!

But this elephant's perfect!
He's easy to groom
I'll clean up his mess
He can live in my room. . .

Pleeeeeeeeeeeeeassse?

Say "Yes"

19

Pretty in Pink

I started yellow, went through blue
and several other colors, too.
Each time I grow, my owner paints
a bigger shell. I've no complaints.
My shell is never dull or drab, for
I'm a rainbow hermit crab!

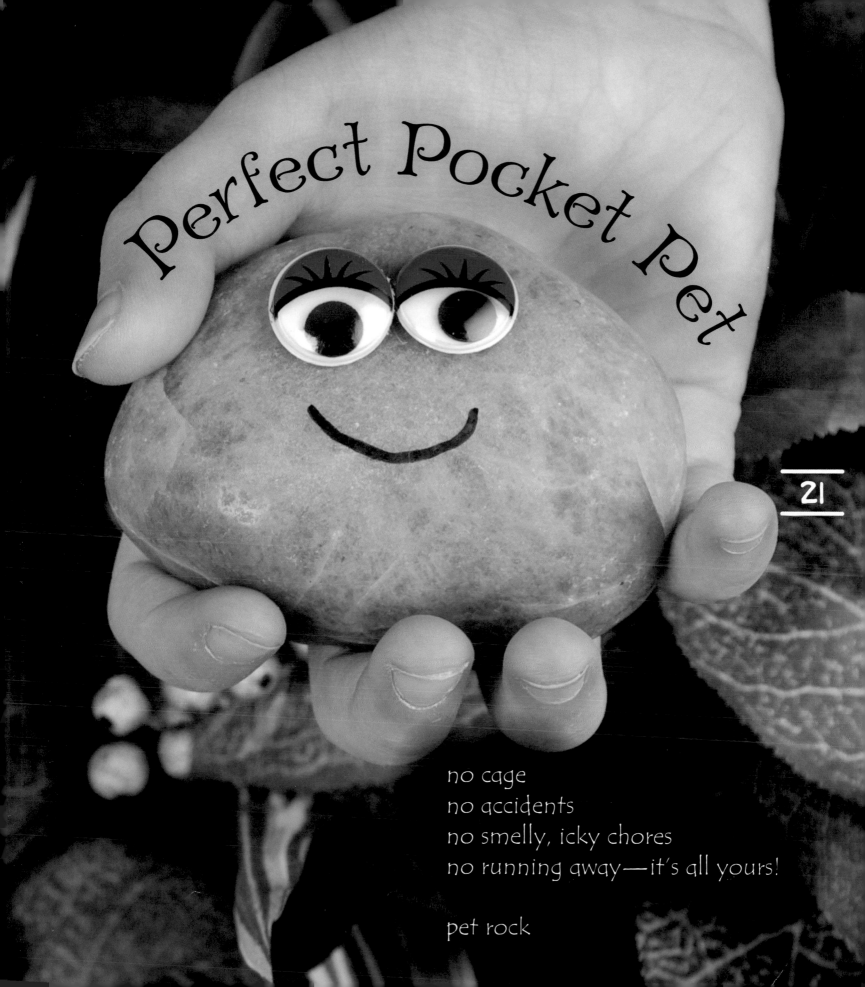

Perfect Pocket Pet

no cage
no accidents
no smelly, icky chores
no running away—it's all yours!

pet rock

Partners

You are bigger than me, but
I always feel safe by your side
    I lead you
    I groom you
    I ride you

but I know the truth —

You take care of me, too

Jumping
for Joy

tail spinning, whipping,
    joy meets toy in mid-air catch:
        leap of summer faith

The Language of Poetry

Couplet — two lines that end with words that rhyme

28

Rhyme — to have an end sound that is the same as the end sound of another word

Rhythm — the pattern of beats in a poem

Simile — to use the word "like" or "as" to say two things are alike

Acrostic

The poem's subject is written straight down the page. Each line of the poem starts with one letter of the word. "A Closer Look" (page 13) is an acrostic poem.

Cinquain

A poem with five lines. The first line has two syllables. The second line has four, the third has six, the fourth has eight, and the last line has two syllables. "Perfect Pocket Pet" (page 21) is an example of a cinquain.

Free Verse

A poem that does not follow a set pattern or rhythm. It often does not rhyme. "Partners" (page 25) is an example of free verse.

Haiku

A short poem that describes a small scene. It has five syllables in the first line, seven syllables in the second line, and five syllables in the third line. "Softness" (page 8) is a haiku.

Limerick

A five-line poem that follows a certain rhythm. The first, second, and fifth lines rhyme, and so do the third and fourth lines. "Friendship Skills: Lesson 1" (page 12) is an example of a limerick.

Glossary

bask (BASK) — to lie or sit in the sun and enjoy it

constant (KON-stuhnt) — happening all the time and never stopping

crave (KRAVE) — to really want something

cushion (KUSH-uhn) — to soften the effect of something

delicate (DEL-uh-kuht) — small, beautiful, and easy to break

drab (DRAB) — dull and ugly

exhaustion (eg-ZAHWS-tuhn) — tiredness

groom (GROOM) — to brush and clean an animal

gruesome (GROO-suhm) — disgusting and horrible

hoverer (HUHV-uhr-ur) — one who floats in one place

iridescent (ih-rih-DES-uhnt) — shiny

lacy (LAY-see) — having a pattern of small holes and delicate stitches

loll (LOL) — to sit or stand in a lazy or relaxed way

mimic (MIM-ik) — to copy

orca (OR-kuh) — a killer whale

sunlamp (SUHN-lamp) — a lamp that gives off light and heat

Read More

Foster, John. *Pet Poems*. New York: Oxford University Press, 2007.

Pearson, Susan. *Who Swallowed Harold? And Other Poems About Pets*. Marshall Cavendish, 2005.

Internet Sites

FactHound offers a safe, fun way to find Internet sites related to this book. All of the sites on FactHound have been researched by our staff.

Here's how:

1. Visit *www.facthound.com*

2. Choose your grade level.

3. Type in this book ID **1429617047** for age-appropriate sites. You may also browse subjects by clicking on letters, or by clicking on pictures and words.

4. Click on the **Fetch It** button.

FactHound will fetch the best sites for you!

Index of Poems

32

A+ Books are published by Capstone Press,
151 Good Counsel Drive, P.O. Box 669, Mankato, Minnesota 56002.
www.capstonepress.com

1 2 3 4 5 6 13 12 11 10 09 08

Library of Congress Cataloging-in-Publication Data
Salas, Laura Purdie.
   A fuzzy-fast blur : poems about pets / by Laura Purdie Salas.
   p. cm. — (A+ books. Poetry)
   Summary: "A collection of original, pet-themed poetry for children accompanied by striking photos. The book demonstrates a variety of common poetic forms and defines poetic devices" — Provided by publisher.
   ISBN-13: 978-1-4296-1704-8 (hardcover)
   ISBN-10: 1-4296-1704-7 (hardcover)
   1. Pets — Juvenile poetry. 2. Animals — Juvenile poetry. 3. Children's poetry, American. I. Title. II. Series.
PS3619.A4256F89 2008
811'.6 — dc22   2008004356

Credits
Jenny Marks, editor; Ted Williams, set designer; Renée T. Doyle, book designer, Wanda Winch, photo researcher

Photo Credits
Capstone Press/Karon Dubke, 2–3, 6–7, 8–9, 10–11, 12, 13, 14–15, 20, 21, 22–23, 24
Corbis/Royalty-Free, 16
Getty Images Inc./UpperCut Images/Cade Martin, 26–27
Shutterstock/Alberto Perez Veiga, 4–5; Hallgerd, 18–19; Martin Valigursky, cover, 1, 28; Nikita Tiunov, 17

Note to Parents, Teachers, and Librarians
A Fuzzy-Fast Blur: Poems about Pets uses colorful photographs and a nonfiction format to introduce children to poetry and pets. This book is designed to be read independently by an early reader or to be read aloud to a pre-reader. The images help early readers and listeners understand the poems and concepts discussed. The book encourages further learning by including the following sections: The Language of Poetry, Glossary, Read More, Internet Sites, and Index of Poems. Early readers may need assistance using these features.